BOEING JETLINERS

D0745287

BOEING JETLINERS

Robbie Shaw

OSPREY
AEROSPACE

First published in Great Britain in 1995
by Osprey, an imprint of Reed Consumer
Books Limited, Michelin House,
81 Fulham Road, London SW3 6RB and
Auckland, Melbourne, Singapore and Toronto.

© Reed International Books 1995

Reprinted 1996

All rights reserved. Apart from any fair
dealing for the purposes of private study,
research, criticism or review, as permitted
under the Copyright, Designs and Patents
Act, 1988, no part of this publication may be
reproduced, stored in a retrieval system, or
transmitted in any form or by any means
electronic, electrical, chemical, mechanical,
optical, photocopying, recording or otherwise,
without prior written permission. All
enquiries should be addressed to the
Publisher.

ISBN 1 85532 528 4

Edited by Tony Holmes
Page design Paul Kime
Produced by Mandarin Offset
Printed and bound in Hong Kong

Front cover Lion Rock provides a
dramatic backdrop for one of six -
300 series 747s operated by Hong
Kong-based Cathay Pacific. Part of
the huge Swire Group, the airline
has 37 747s in use, or on order

Back cover A China Southern
Airlines 737-300 lines up on Kai
Tak's runway, prior to commencing
its return flight to mainland China.
This airline is the biggest operator of
737s in the region, boasting a fleet of
40 'baby Boeings', most of which are
leased

Title page There is no doubt that the
Boeing Airplane Company is the
most successful manufacturer of jet
airliners, and its products can be
seen in virtually every corner of the
globe. One of Boeing's best and most
faithful customers is British Airways
(BA), whose first Washington state
product was the 707, which entered
service with the airline in 1960.
There are those who claim, with
some justification, that the letters
'BA' actually mean Boeing Always,
and it certainly is a mystery as to
why the airline shuns Airbus
products. Even the ten Airbus A320s
currently flying in the airline's livery
were reluctantly inherited from the
take-over of British Caledonian. In
this shot a row of British Airways
747s of various series are being
readied for their next flights from
London Heathrow's Terminal 4. The
three aircraft nearest the camera
illustrate all three Jumbo variants in
use with the airline – series -100,
-200 and -400

For a catalogue of all books published by Osprey Aerospace
please write to:

**The Marketing Department, Reed Books,
3rd Floor, Michelin House, 81 Fulham Road, London SW3 6RB**

Foreword

Over the last four decades the Boeing Airplane Company has proved to be the world's most successful manufacturer of jet airliners, starting with the 707 – the aircraft which it can be claimed revolutionised transatlantic travel – and progressing over four decades through to the 777, which is about to enter service as these words are written. Boeing currently has no less than five jet airliner types in production, the 737, 747, 757, 767 and 777, and this book takes a look at these aircraft in current service in their natural habitats – the international airports of the world from Amsterdam to Auckland, from Hong Kong to Honolulu and from Rio to Reykjavik.

Over the following pages the photo-captions will feature designations such as Boeing 747-136, so for those not familiar with company production numbers some explanation is necessary. In the 1950s Boeing assigned each new customer an individual two-digit designation number, but when they ran out of these some years ago it incorporated a number/letter combination. British Airways, for instance, is '36', so the 747 series -100s, -200s and -400s of the airline are designated 747-136, -236 and -436 respectively. Eva Air was a later customer and its designation is '5E', meaning that its 747-400s are designated as 747-45Es.

Unless otherwise credited, all photographs were taken by the author using Nikon F801S cameras (and associated lenses) loaded with Kodachrome 64 film. Finally, I would like to take this opportunity to thank my wife Eileen for her unstinting support and invaluable proof-reading.

Robbie Shaw
May 1995.

Contents

Left The least successful variant of the 747 was the SP model, only 44 of which were built. This particular aircraft, N4508H, was delivered to China Airlines in September 1981, and although allocated the registration B-1882, this has never been taken up. The aircraft is currently operated by China Airlines subsidiary, Mandarin Airlines, and was photographed at Hong Kong's Kai Tak airport operating a Taipei service on behalf of the parent company in November 1994

The Boeing Airplane Company

Until the advent of the 707 Boeing was undoubtedly better known for its series of heavy bombers built before, during and after World War 2. Types like the B-17, B-29, B-47 and B-52 were built in their thousands, and a spin off from these projects was the experience accrued by the Company in the construction of large, multi-engined, aircraft – experience that eventually resulted in the world's airliner behemoth, the 747. However, before we take a closer look at just how the Jumbo evolved, let us briefly chart the history of the company which is now the world's largest airliner manufacturer.

Prior to the formation of the Boeing Company, William E Boeing and a colleague, Naval Officer Conrad Westervelt, designed and built a biplane they christened the B&W, after their own initials, in Washington state. However, prior to the aircraft being completed Westervelt was transferred to the East Coast and had to relinquish his role. Only two B&Ws were built, both of which were ultimately sold to the New Zealand Government. The first aircraft built exclusively by Boeing was the Model 40A biplane, which was produced in early 1927 for use on US Mail contract flights, and was actually operated by the Boeing Air Transport Company. This aircraft had a cruising speed of 105 mph and a range of 650 miles (1046 km). Almost 70 years later the company's flagship, the 747-400, is capable of speeds up to 615 mph, and is endowed with an incredible range of 8406 miles (7300 nm / 13,528 km). A quick comparison of the two Boeings allows you to appreciate the strides made in aviation over the past seven decades.

Right The largest variant of the Boeing 737 currently in use is the series-400. This stretched version of the series-300 can normally seat a maximum of 170 passengers, although some charter operators have managed to squeeze in a few more. The 737 is currently the world's best-selling airliner, with some 3100 delivered at the time of writing – a record unlikely ever to be equalled. The aircraft illustrated is 737-400 F-GFUG of French charter operator Corsair, easily identified by its tail livery, a la Kandinsky!

The Model 40A was followed by the improved Model 40B, which was capable of carrying four passengers and 500lb of mail, and a total of 77 were built. The company had the foresight to see that air travel was to be the mode of transport of the future, and the Model 40A was superseded by the three-engined Model 80 biplane, with a capacity for 12 passengers. Still looking to the future, it wasn't long before a more powerful and lengthened variant was introduced, which duly became Model 80A with capacity increased to 18 passengers. Even at this early stage, however, Boeing found that the aviation business could be a cut throat one and, as Fokker and Ford had stole a lead with similar machines, the Model 80A was produced in very small numbers. It does, however, feature in the annals of aviation history as it was on this type that Boeing Air Transport claim to have been the first airline to introduce stewardesses to provide in-flight cabin service. A pure freight variant of the Model 80A was the Model 95.

In 1930 Boeing produced its first all-metal aircraft, the Model 200 Monomail. As the name suggests this was a monoplane with retractable landing gear, which was quite an innovation at the time. It was, however, purely a 'mail plane' with no room for passengers, although this was later rectified in the Model 221, which provided cramped seating for six.

The first major commercial success for Boeing was the twin-engined, low wing, monoplane Model 247, capable of transporting ten passengers coast to coast in under 20 hours, with seven en-route stops. The 247 featured several innovations for airliners of that period such as heating, sound proofing and a toilet. Whilst the type was still on the drawing boards United Airlines placed an order for 60 of the type – an order of such magnitude was unheard of in those days ! The one drawback of this large order, however, was that other airlines who wanted the 247 would have to wait until United's aircraft had been delivered. Most, such as TWA and Eastern, looked elsewhere particularly to Douglas and the DC-1. The successor to the latter was the DC-2, and to compete with it Boeing offered the improved Model 247D, although it wasn't a match for the Douglas product. In 1938 Boeing came up with the idea of the Model 307 Stratoliner, a derivative of the B-17, and the type's maiden flight was made on the last day of 1938. The 307 was the first pressurised airliner in service, making its debut with TWA in 1940. It went on to reduce the flight time from Los Angeles to New York to just over 12 hours, with only one en-route stop.

Two months later Pan American introduced the type on services from Miami to South America, although just over a year later these aircraft were pressed into military service as the United States entered World War 2. Due to the conflict monopolising all production efforts, only ten Model 307s were ever built. Another aircraft whose career suffered due to the War was the Model 314 Clipper. This large four-engined flying boat was developed specifically to meet a Pan American requirement. It was truly a giant of its

Above Taxying to the gate at Auckland's Jean Batten International Terminal is ZK-NBH *Awatere*, one of 12 767s in use with Air New Zealand. This particular aircraft is a 767-209(ER) built in 1983, and it previously served with China Airlines as B-1838 until acquired by the Kiwi national carrier in December 1989. The Maori name Awatere translates to 'swift flowing river'

day, and could carry up to 74 passengers in luxurious surroundings over a range of 3500 miles. Only 12 Clippers were built, and the type entered transatlantic service in 1939, linking New York with Southampton and Marseilles. These services, however, were soon suspended due to the outbreak of the War, and ultimately the Clippers, like their Model 247 cousins, were impressed into military service.

The next, and last of the piston-engined airliners to be built by Boeing, was the classic Model 377 Stratocruiser. The 'Strat', as it was fondly referred to, was a derivative of the military C-97 Stratofreighter, 888 of which were built for the US Air Force – many of these were later converted into tanker aircraft. The Model 377 pioneered transatlantic travel as airlines such as Pan American and BOAC introduced them during 1949. It had a number of features which influenced the designers of the 747. Up to 100 passengers could be accommodated in the 'double-bubble' fuselage, which featured two decks connected by a spiral staircase that led to the lower deck lounge and bar. Although an engineering success, due to competition from the DC-6 and Lockheed Constellation, only 56 civil 'Strat's were built. Boeing's next product brought the dawn of a new era – THE JET AGE.

Boeing 707

Boeing's first jets were the B-47 Stratojet and the eight-engined B-52 Stratofortress bombers – the latter is still in frontline service today. The company's premier jet airliner can rightly be described as the aircraft which changed intercontinental air travel forever. The Boeing 707 first flew on 20 December 1957 and, with massive orders for its C-135 military derivative, the future looked assured for the Boeing Company. Ultimately over 800 C-135s were produced in a number of variants, the bulk of which were KC-135 tankers – many of these are still in use today, though most have been re-engined with the French CFM-56 powerplant.

Initially, airline orders for the 707 were sluggish, but once Pan American committed to an initial batch of 20 and duly put them into service, operators rushed to buy the aircraft. The 707 became the world's third jet airliner behind the de Havilland Comet and Tupolev Tu-104, both of which were already in service.

The main competitor to the 707 was the Douglas DC-8, as early structural problems with the Comet ruled it out, whilst a later British challenger in the form of the Vickers VC10 was hamstrung from the beginning by an apathetic and disinterested launch customer in the form of BOAC – less than 50 VC10s were eventually built.

The initial 707 was the -120 series, which entered service with Pan American on 26 October 1958, and was soon introduced on the New York - London route in competition with the Comet 4s of BOAC. This variant of 707 lacked the range for such long sectors, however, and had to frequently

Left The 707 is now in the twilight of its career as it approaches its fourth decade in service, and numbers of the fuel-thirsty machine in airworthy condition are dwindling fast. There is one continent, however, where the type is becoming more prevalent – Africa. There seems to be no end to the number of airlines (many of them new) which operate this venerable aircraft in the cargo role, and as more and more of them venture into Europe, it has been observed that the maintenance records for some of their 707s are dubious to say the very least. Illustrated is 707-324C freighter D2-TOK operated by Angola Air Charter

make refuelling stops en-route. It was more far better suited to transcontinental routes, which it successfully served in the colours of American and National Airlines. A longer range version known as the -320 or -420 series, depending on engine type, was dubbed the 707 Intercontinental, and proved to be extremely popular with national carriers the world over. Ironically, the -420, powered by Rolls-Royce Conway engines, was selected by BOAC in deference to the home-grown VC10, and the type duly replaced the airline's Comet 4s on transatlantic and long-haul services. An improved version of the Pratt & Whitney JT3C engine, known as the JT3D-1, offering a significant increase in power and a corresponding decrease in fuel consumption, was also ushered in at this point. Aircraft fitted with such engines had the suffix B added to their designation.

The most popular 707 variants proved to be the -320B and -320C, the latter being a passenger/cargo convertible which has a large side-loading

Above During the eary part of 1994 Angola Air Charter 707 freighters were a frequent sight at European airports. Although wearing Angola Air Charter titles, 707-324C D2-TON was still wearing TAAG Angola Airlines livery when photographed in January 1994

Above The number of African 707 cargo operators flourishes, particularly in Nigeria, and one of the latest to acquire the type is Lagos based ADC Airlines, which has added a small number to its modest inventory of BAC One-Elevens and DC-9s. Illustrated is 5N-BBD, an aircraft which previously served with Qantas and British Midland

Above Air Gambia was formed in 1991 with the aim of providing a Banjul -
London/Gatwick service, and it chose to lease a trio of 707s based at
Manston, in Kent, Leased from Omega Aviation, initially with Liberian
registrations, the 707s were later transferred to the Gambian register, but
soon afterward this occurred the airline had to temporarily cease operations.
The Gatwick service is now operated by an Ethiopian Airlines Boeing 757 on
behalf of Air Gambia. Illustrated is 707-323B C5-GOA, which was previously
registered as EL-AKC

Above Nigeria Airways was formed in September 1971 to operate services previously undertaken by the West African Airways Corporation (Nigeria), and it initially employed three 707s on its intercontinental routes. The current fleet comprises eight 737s, four Airbus A310s and two McDonnell-Douglas DC-10s. Only one of the 707-3F9Cs – 5N-ABK– is still operational, performing freight services. Here it seen at Gatwick on 1 November 1994

Above Looking as new as the day it was built, 1975-vintage 707-3L6C A6-HRM displays United Arab Emirates titles on its fuselage. This aircraft was the 900th 707 built, and it is today operated as a VIP aircraft by the government of Dubai, and in whose service it uses the callsign 'Falcon One'. Note the immaculate finish on the cowlings of the Pratt & Whitney JT3D-7(Q) engines

Right Formerly known as Alia, Royal Jordanian Airlines has operated 707s since January 1971. Although three of the type are still in operational use, today they are used purely in the cargo role, whilst international services are undertaken by Airbus A310s and Lockheed L-1011 Tristars. Illustrated soon after take-off is 707-324C JY-AJL, complete with gold 'Cargo' titles on its black livery

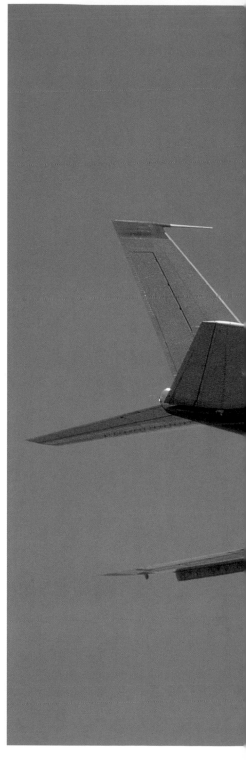

freight door on the forward fuselage. This variant also featured a longer wing, slotted leading-edge flaps and extended trailing edge flaps to improve performance and handling capabilities. A slightly lighter and less powerful variant of the 707, known as the 720, was also produced in the early 1960s, but failed to have the same success as its big brother – only 65 were sold. No less than 1010 707s were built, a production run which, at the time, entitled the type to be written into the record books as the most successful jet airliner. Later still the basic 707 airframe was used as a mount for the radar on the E-3 Sentry AWACS. At the time of writing there are still 135 707s in global use, many with freight operators in the Third World.

Above Seldom seen and rarely photographed in western Europe are aircraft of Khartoum-based Trans Arabian Air Transport (TAAT). The company operates two Antonov An-26s and three 707s in the freight role, all of which are leased. ST-ANP is a 1967-vintage 707-351C which the company acquired early in 1994. Note the DC-8 freighter in the background, a type that TAAT operated several year ago

Above Shanghai Airlines was the first independent operator in the People's Republic of China, and it began operations in 1986 with three 707s. Two of these are seen here on the ramp at Shanghai's Hongqiao airport, in company with another Boeing product, the Model 234 – the commercial variant of the Chinook – which was on a sales demonstration tour of China at the time this photo was taken. Shanghai Airlines now operates a modern fleet of 757s and 767s

Boeing 727

Before the 707 had even entered service Boeing was already looking at the prospect of producing a short- to medium-haul jet airliner to complement its four-engined model. Given the designation 727, the aircraft featured a fuselage with the same width as the 707, thus giving operators a degree of commonality in cabin interiors for the two types. The design of the remainder of the aircraft, however, was a significant deviation from previous concepts, being both a tri-jet and incorporating a swept-back 'T' tail, the base of which included the intake for the third engine. The jetpipe for this engine was in the tail cone, with the other two engines mounted on the rear fuselage. The Pratt & Whitney JT8D was the powerplant selected, in preference to the originally favoured Allison engine which was a license-built Rolls-Royce Spey. In December 1960 Boeing authorised production of the 727 following the receipt of a launch orders for 40 aircraft apiece from Eastern and United Airlines. The initial variant was the 727-100, which could carry up to 125 passengers in maximum configuration.

The prototype took to the skies for the first time on 9 February 1963, exactly 13 months after the maiden flight of its nearest rival the Hawker-Siddeley Trident – the latter bore a remarkable resemblance to the Boeing product! A year later Eastern, and then United, inaugurated commercial services with the aircraft, followed later in the month by the delivery of the first export aircraft to Lufthansa. As the delivery rate increased Boeing soon overhauled the Trident's lead in the battle for tri-jet orders primarily because the American product could haul a larger payload over a greater distance.

Increasing engine thrust by Pratt & Whitney encouraged Boeing to offer other variants of the 727, including the 727C, a passenger/cargo combi variant. This featured the same forward fuselage side-loading freight door

Left Despite its age the 727 is still present in large numbers in the fleets of US airlines. Delta operates the largest fleet of 727s in the world, with over 130 series -200s in its inventory, and in a bid to reduce the high fuel burn of the type, they have had two its aircraft fitted with winglets for a trial period. Photographed as it turns onto the runway at Miami airport is 727-232 N515DA, which was built in 1978

as on the 707-320C, and an innovative feature which permitted seats to be mounted on pallets allowing quick conversion from passenger to all-freight configuration. The latter was known as the QC (Quick Change) variant.

The most significant occurrence in the development of the 727, however, was the idea to stretch the fuselage through the insertion of two 6.1 m (20 ft) plugs fore and aft of the wings, thus permitting a substantial increase in capacity to 189 passengers. Launch customer for this popular variant was Northwest Airlines, and the type's maiden flight took place on 27 July 1967. This model has operated in the colours of virtually every major American carrier over the decades, and many are still plying their trade back and forth across the United States. In the early 1970s Boeing went even further in the tri-jet's development with the 727-200 Advanced, which featured more powerful engines, a higher fuel capacity and an increase in

Above Another US carrier with large fleet of Boeing aircraft is United Airlines. Their current 727-200 fleet comprises some 75 aircraft, and until recently a small number of these were based in mainland Europe for use as feeder liners, carrying long-haul passengers in to and out of Heathrow. Photographed about to land at the aforementioned airport is 25-year-old 727-222 N7642U, an aircraft which is presently stored in California

Above American Trans Air operates a fleet of 727s, 757s and Tristars primarily in the charter market, and in this capacity it frequently operates flights on behalf of the US military. Fulfilling work of this nature are a small number of 727s based in Europe, which are used for inter-theatre passenger flights for the US Air Force. The airline's 727 fleet comprises 16 leased aircraft formerly operated by Alaska Airlines and USAir. 727-264 N763AT previously served with the latter operator as N763US

gross weight. In the middle of the decade the company considered further improvements to the 727, including a projected series -300 with a further increase in fuselage length, but these were abandoned in favour of the all-new model 7N7, which is now known as the 757.

When Boeing launched the 727 the company stated that it expected orders for some 300+ aircraft, and never in their wildest dreams could they have imagined that when production finally ceased in August 1984 following the delivery of the the last aircraft to Federal Express, an amazing 1832 would have been built. Despite the innovative autoland blind landing system which was perfected by the Trident in British Airways service, and which enabled the type to fly in poor visibility whilst other types remained on the ground, sales of the Trident reached just 117 examples.

Due to the introduction of newer types from Airbus and Boeing, the 727 is now a rare sight in Europe. However, the type is still plentiful in the home market, and is becoming increasingly popular in South America. Some 727s have been hush-kitted to meet more stringent noise regulations, whilst Delta and Canada's Royal Aviation have fitted winglets to improve fuel consumption, thus ensuring a future for the type into the 21st century.

Above Towards the end of 1990 Air Canada began disposing of its fleet of
727s, the majority of which were sold to Federal Express for service on their
night mail/freight routes. The Canadian operator took delivery of 36 727-233s
in the late 1960s and early 70s, and used them both on domestic and cross-
border services to the USA. Wearing airline's original livery, 727-233
C-GYNG was photographed on short finals to runway 24L at Toronto's
Lester B Pearson airport in May 1989

Left Northwest Airlines is another major US operator of the 727, still utilising
56 aircraft, including some previously operated by Eastern and Republic
Airlines. Photographed taxying past an Air Canada 767 is Northwest Boeing
727-251 N256US. This shot was taken in May 1989, prior to the introduction
of Northwest's current livery

Above Air Transat was formed in 1986, and from its Montreal base it operates charter flights to Europe, Florida and the Caribbean. European services are flown primarily to France and the UK by five L-1011 Tristars and four Boeing 757s. The company also has three former Air Canada 727-233s which were taken on charge in May and June of 1991. Parked at the gate at Toronto's Terminal 1 is C-GAAG

Right One of Canada's newest charter operators was formed in 1991 under the name Royal Airlines, and it received its first aircraft – a former Dan-Air 727 – in January of the following year. For some reason the airline has now changed its name to Royal Aviation, although only the first word appears on the titles painted on its aircraft. The company now has six 727s, five of which have seen service with Dan-Air, whilst the sixth is an ex-Sterling machine. The company also has two Tristars, and these are used on transatlantic services. Not long after Delta fitted winglets to two of its 727s – and prior to the results of the trial being published – Royal added similar aerodynamic devices to 727-212 C-FRYS. The aircraft in question is seen outside Canadian's maintenance hangar at Toronto in June 1994 – it had previously served with Dan-Air as G-BHVT

Above left The number of 727s based in Europe is diminishing rapidly, partly as a result of the type's now uneconomical fuel consumption, but also due to the strong noise-sensitive environmental lobby in many countries in the region. Even before its unfortunate demise, Dan-Air was actively trying to dispose of its fleet of 727-200s which it had operated for years to many European holiday destinations, including Geneva (where 727-264 G-BMLP was snapped) during the short ski season. This particular machine now serves with Royal Aviation

Left Photographed as it rotates from runway 24 at Amsterdam's Schiphol airport, Lufthansa 727-230 D-ABKT was just one of 34 Boeing tri-jets the airline operated from 1964 to 1993. Lufthansa was the first European customer for the 727, and this photograph of D-ABKT is rather rare as this was the only one of its type to appear in the airline's current livery, which has dispensed with the once familiar dark blue cheatline

Above Although it has received a number of new aircraft such as the A320 and MD-87 over the past few years, Spanish flag carrier Iberia still operates a sizeable fleet of 30 727-200s. The airline is currently taking delivery of 757s, although rumour has it that its eight brand new A321s also on order are to be cancelled. At the time of writing Iberia finds itself in a perilous position, suffering mounting losses and plagued by a militant workforce who refuse to implement any restructuring plans put forward by the management. Posing at Las Palmas in Iberia's bright and prominent livery is 727-236 EC-CBD *Murcia*

Above Coming in 'over the fence' for a landing on runway 10 at Granada is Iberia's EC-CBC. Although situated at the foothills of the Sierra Nevada mountains, 580 m (1860 ft) above sea level, Granada poses no problems to the 727. Note the 'in-line' position of all three engines

Left Denmark's Sterling Airways had long been the country's leading charter operator, and it came as something of a surprise to the industry when the airline ceased operations in September 1993 due to financial problems. One of the last major European operators of the Caravelle, Sterling steadily supplemented its fleet of French airliners with a fleet of 727s throughout the late 1970s and early 80s. In 1994 the airline was reborn under the title Sterling European Airlines, equipped with six of its original 727s, although they are now painted in a totally new blue and white livery, as seen on 727-2J4 OY-SAU. Note the markings on the engine nacelle proclaiming it to be a 'Silent 727' – a misnomer if ever I heard one!

Above One of the newest 727 operators is Azerbaijan Airlines, which utilises two leased series -236 aircraft acquired in December 1992 and March 1993. Prior to it becoming independent of the USSR, the company operated as the Azerbaijan Directorate of Aeroflot, so hence it still operates a predominantly Soviet-built fleet of Antonov An-26s and -32s, Tupolev Tu-134s and -154s and Yakovlev Yak-40s. The airline has adopted a very attractive livery, as seen in this shot of the company's first 727, 4K-AZ1. Note the letters AHY on the rear fuselage which stand for Azerbaijan Hava Yollari – this loosely translates to mean 'Azerbaijan Airlines' in the local Turkic dialect

Above Genius Air was a brief operator of the 727, using YU-AKE (727-2H9) of the politically crippled Jugoslovenski Aerotransport (JAT) for a short period in 1992. The aircraft was photographed at Luton airport whilst operating a football supporters' charter flight

Above Yemenia was the national carrier of North Yemen, and from its base at Sana'a, operated a fleet of 727s on a prosperous schedule of regional and European flights. However, after many years of tension South and North Yemen united as one country in May 1990, but after just four years of union civil war broke out, and for a few months the airline ceased international operations. These have now recommenced using its pre-war fleet of five 727s – that is assuming that none have been destroyed during the hostilities. Illustrated is 727-2N8 7O-ACY which, prior to unification, was registered as 4W-ACI

Left Libyan Arab Airlines is the 'leper' of the international commercial aviation scene due to the government of that country refusing to hand over those suspected of the planting the bomb which destroyed the Pan-American 747 over Lockerbie on 21 December 1988. The United Nations has imposed a ban on all flights in to or out of the country, and apart from a few domestic services, this has effectively grounded the airline. Libyan Arab currently has nine 727s, the first of which was acquired in 1971 as a replacement for the Caravelle. This 727-2L5, registered 5A-DIF, was photographed on approach to Athens prior to the country becoming the pariah that it is now

Boeing 737

The decision to build the Boeing 737 was announced on 19 February 1965, and exactly 25 years later it entered the record books as the 1833rd of the type was rolled out at Boeing's Renton plant, destined for British Midland Airways. This aircraft ensured that the 737 became the world's best-selling commercial jet, a title previously bestowed on its elder cousin, the 727. Amazingly, 30 years after the green light was given to commence type production, humble 'little' 737s are still being churned out by Boeing, with the current order book containing some 3053 separate entries, of which over 2500 have been delivered.

The premier variant of the 737 was the series -100, which first flew on 9 April 1967 – launch customer Lufthansa received its first 737 eight months later, becoming the first foreign airline to serve as the launch customer for a US airliner in the process. The 737-100 featured a conventional tail unit, unlike its 'T' tail competitors, the BAC One-Eleven and DC-9, and it was designed to carry 100 passengers.

Only 30 of this variant were produced as production soon switched to the larger and more powerful -200, which featured a fuselage lengthened by only 1.82 m (6 ft) – despite this modest stretch the -200 was capable of accommodating a further 30 passengers. Launch customer for this variant was United Airlines, and although sales were initially sluggish, the -200 eventually proved to be an extremely popular aircraft. It soon became standard equipment for many of Europe's increasing number of charter airlines, including Britannia Airways, and like the 727 was also available in QC combi fit.

Left Despite its codesharing link with British Airways, USAir is still suffering severe, and seemingly endless, financial losses. The airline has also unfortunately been in the public eye over a serious of fatal crashes in the last few years. Despite these setbacks, USAir still has a large and varied fleet of in excess of 400 aircraft, not including the many commuter turboprops which are operated under the USAir Express banner by nine commuter airlines. The most numerous type in the airline's inventory is the 737, with over 200 of three different variants in use. These include 54 series -4B7 aircraft, one of which (N778AU) is seen here approaching its gate at Toronto's Terminal 1

Above The 737 is manufactured at the company's Renton plant in the suburbs of Seattle. When an aircraft first emerges it is finished in a greenish-coloured layer of primer to prevent corrosion. The rudder, however, has to be painted prior to being fitted to the aircraft, so providing you know your airline liveries, you can identify the customer. All 737s appear to be test flown in the same registration, N1786B, so for aircraft spotters this can be very confusing, not to mention downright frustrating, as there can frequently be five or six aircraft parked outside the plant all wearing the same identity! On the subject of identities, this 737-300 entering the runway at Renton for taxy trials is destined to serve with Southwest Airlines

Right The tail markings of Hawaiian carrier Aloha Airlines glow like a sunburst in the fading evening light

Left Since the previous photograph was taken Aloha Airlines has introduced an impressive new livery as featured here on the airline's first series -400 aircraft, 737-497 N401AL. The aircraft was delivered in November 1992, and is photographed at Honolulu two months later whilst taxying for departure from the 'reef' runway

Above Despite deliveries of Airbus A320s, Canadian Airlines International still operates a substantial fleet of almost 50 737s. All are all series -200 aircraft which had seen service with airlines such as Canadian Pacific, Pacific Western and Quebecair. The identities of the previous owners are usually obvious from the registrations. In this case 737-275 C-GMPW was previously operated in the colours of Pacific Western. This aircraft is one of two which carry the 'Vacances Canadien' titles or, as it says in English on the other side, 'Canadian Holidays'. It is interesting to see that the difficult, potentially contentious 'a/e' decision about Anglo-French spelling has been partly avoided by the use of the logo!

The 737-200 Advanced featured the use of graphite composites to reduce the weight of the airframe, which in turn increased the maximum payload. The last of 1114 series -200s was delivered to China in August 1988, and of this total 19 were bought by the USAF as T-43A navigation trainers, whilst three special surveillance variants were also acquired by the TNI-AU (Indonesian Air Force). The type is also in use with several other air arms as a VIP transport.

Above Brazil's Rio Sul is a subsidiary of the national carrier Varig. Its modest fleet is made up of Embraer EMB-120 Brasilias and Fokker 50s, although it has recently acquired four 737-500 aircraft which carry the inscription 'Boeing 737-500 Regional' behind the front passenger door. Photographed against a pretty impressive background at Rio de Janeiro's downtown Santos Dumont airport is 737-5Y0 PP-SLT. This aircraft was delivered to the airline in January 1994

Left Varig Airlines uses a sizeable fleet of 737s, including 17 series -200s and 26 -300s, with more of the latter on order. The aircraft featured here at Campo Grande airport (PP-CJO) is a 737-2C3 series, which was built in 1974 and acquired by Varig in 1993 from the now defunct Cruzeiro

Current production centres on three 'new generation' variants, the series -300, -400 and -500. The go-ahead for the series -300 was given in March 1981 following orders from USAir and Southwest Airlines. The latter carrier currently operates over 150 737s, with many more on order. All 'new generation' 737s are powered by CFM56 engines which are not only more powerful and fuel efficient, but considerably quieter than those used on the earlier models. All three types have a common wing span, which is a slight increase on the -200, and all have a standardised two-man cockpits, featuring advanced avionics. Amazingly, all five also have identical fuselage width and height dimensions. The fuselage length of the series -300 has been increased by almost 3.05 m (10 ft), giving a typical mixed

capacity of 128 passengers, with a maximum capacity of 149. The first 737-300 flew on 24 February 1984, and by the end of the decade almost 1000 of the type had been ordered. Of the three variants currently in production, the -300 is presently the best-seller.

The introduction of the -400 brought an even longer fuselage into the family, thanks to a 'plug' of 3.05 m (10 ft) being inserted which took the jet's overall length to 36.4 m (119 ft 7 in). In a mixed layout this provides seating for 146 passengers, which can be increased to 170 in charter configuration. Right from the start the new -400 had the makings of a winner following an initial order for 25 aircraft from Piedmont, plus of course a rash of orders from the increasing numbers of leasing companies across the globe. The 1000th 'new generation' 737 built was the first -400 for British Airways, and it was duly delivered to the airline on 16 October 1991.

Above One of Varig's newer 'baby Boeings' is this 737-341, registered PP-VPB, which was delivered to the airline in July 1992. The aircraft was photographed in October 1994 at Santos Dumont, the compact downtown airport for Rio de Janeiro which was built on reclaimed land and has a single runway surrounded on three sides by water

Above British Airways joined the 737 club when it received the first of its series -200 aircraft in 1980. Only 15 of these remain with the airline's mainline division, most of which operate from Gatwick. The rest have been transferred to the Birmingham and Manchester regional divisions. The airline also operates a substantial fleet of 24 series -400s, plus a further 12 acquired following the take-over of the lamented Dan-Air. One of the latter machines, 737-4Q8 G-BSNW, is illustrated at rest after a hard day's work

Above 737-4YO G-UKLB belongs to Air UK Leisure, although when this photograph was taken in May 1993 it was operating a London - Athens service on behalf of South East European Airways – a new Greek operator. The Greek airline operates the service under a Virgin Atlantic Airways franchise agreement which sees the latter assisting in marketing and sales, as well as allowing its livery to be painted on the aircraft. This 737 has since been returned to its owner and replaced by an Airbus A320

Right Formerly known as Gibair, GB Airways is actually based at London/Gatwick, from whence it operates services to Gibraltar and North Africa. The company also has scheduled services from Heathrow, and has just announced that it is to become a British Airways franchise operator, whereby its aircraft and crews will soon appear in BA livery and uniforms. This is just the latest of a number of British airlines which have been virtually swallowed up by the monolithic carrier, making a mockery of the British government's policy of encouraging competition. The Mergers and Monopolies Commission failed to act when BA bought out both British Caledonian and Dan-Air, and not surprisingly is remaining silent and innefective now

Above Aer Lingus is one of the very few carriers which can claim to have operated virtually every variant of the 737 built so far, the series -100 being the only type not to have appeared in the airline's livery. The Irish flag carrier took delivery of its first 737-200s in 1969, and although some still remain on the inventory today, they are either aircraft currently out on lease or up for sale. The airline's 737 present fleet comprises two series -300s, six -400s and ten series -500s. One of the latter is EI-CDC, a 737-548 named *St Munchin* which was photographed at Shannon

Left 'Holiday Boeings'. Two aircraft from two of Britain's most successful holiday charter airlines taxy for departure – an Air 2000 757 on the left and an Air UK Leisure 737-400 to the right

By the mid-1980s, although still popular, the series -200 was a 25-year-old design and, compared with the technology of the -300, was becoming outdated. The obvious solution was a variant that combined the fuselage dimensions of the -200 with the technology of the -300 – hence the series -500 was born, which promised to be 25 per cent more fuel efficient than the elderly -200. The prototype took-off from Renton on 30 June 1989, and the first production jet was delivered to Southwest on 28 February 1990. By this time 193 series -500s had been ordered by 19 airlines.

An important milestone in the career of the 737 and Lufthansa occurred on 25 February 1991 when the 2000th 737 built was handed over to the German operator. This became the 100th 737 received by Lufthansa in 23

Above Air Berlin operates a fleet of six 737-400s on behalf of German tour operators, and its aircraft are a common sight at the popular Mediterranean and Canary Islands holiday airports. Ilustrated is 737-46J D-ABAE, and when photographed in November 1993 the company had a fleet of five aircraft, four of which were on the ground at Las Palmas. To help promote Berlin's bid for the 2000 Olympics the airline's aircraft sported 'Berlin 2000' titles and the city's logo of the face of a smiling bear – after Berlin lost its bid to host the event, on one aircraft at least the bear's smile was changed to a frown! At the time of writing Boeing have just announced that Air Berlin has placed an order for six new 737-800s

Left A long-established customer of Douglas aircraft, KLM now operates sizeable fleets of Boeing 737s and 747s. The camera has caught 737-306 PH-BDK following rotation from Amsterdam Sciphol's runway 24

years. During 1991 Boeing delivered an incredible 215 737s, setting a record for the most commercial aircraft of a single type to be delivered in a year.

As part of its ongoing process to further enhance its product, Boeing has announced plans for the 'next generation' 737 which will feature a redesigned passenger cabin and improved flight deck instrumentation. Initially it will produce two new variants, the 737-700 and -800. The former is a 144-seat aircraft equivalent to the -300, and its launch operator was one of Boeing's best customers – Southwest Airlines – who, in January 1994 ordered an incredible 63 aircraft. The first European customer for this

Above Amsterdam-based Air Holland is a small charter company with a fleet of two 737s and two 757s. One of the former, 737-3L9 PH-OZA, is illustrated as it unsticks from the runway at Schiphol.

Above right Each summer for the past few years the Norwegian independent airline Braathens has painted an aircraft in special 'Sommerflyet' markings designed by children. A close up of the 1993 scheme is seen here on 737-505 LN-BRX. Note the name and age of the child who has devised each individual piece of artwork.

Right The 1994 'Sommerflyet' scheme was applied to 737-505 LN-BRJ in July, and this photograph was taken soon afterwards. These markings are usually removed at the end of the summer, but LN-BRJ was seen in late December 1994 with special 'Olympiaflyet' markings!

Above Founded in 1988 as TEA Basel, this Swiss charter operator has recently changed its name to TEA Switzerland, with the latter word now prominent in the fuselage titling. Four 737-300s are operated, including 737-3YO HB-IID which still bears the name *City of Hanoi*, a legacy from its period of lease to Vietnam Airlines

Right Maersk Air operates both domestic and international scheduled services, as well as inclusive tour charter flights from both Billund and Copenhagen using a fleet of Fokker 50s and 737s. International scheduled services are operated by three 737-500s, with a further two having been leased to Korea's Asiana, though one has subsequently been lost in a fatal crash. The 737s used on charter flights are -300 and -400 series aircraft. Maersk's soothing two-tone blue livery is seen here on 737-5L9 OY-MAE

variant is Denmark's Maersk Air, who have placed an order for six aircraft – the type will be delivered from 1997. Seating 164 to 189 passengers, the series -800 is a stretched version of the 737-400, with the fuselage lengthened by 2.78 m (9 ft 2 in). Deliveries will commence in 1998 to German charter operators Air Berlin and Hapag-Lloyd, who have ordered six and 16 respectively.

The Boeing 737 success story just seems to go on and on, and it's not inconceivable that the number built will ultimately reach 4000 – a figure which is extremely unlikely ever to be equalled.

Above One of the more striking liveries seen in recent years is that of Portuguese charter specialist Air Columbus, whose fleet of 727s and 737s are regularly sighted at British airports. At the time of writing, however, most of its aircraft are now devoid of markings, which may be connected to the airline's reported financial difficulties. Illustrated in full livery is 737-33A CS-TKC, an aircraft which previously served with the now defunct Norway Airlines

Left The Polish national carrier LOT (Polskie Linie Lotnicze) has recently acquired 737s to replace Tu-134s and -154s on European services. Until it received the five -500s and four -400s it had on order, the airline leased -500s from Swedish carrier Linjeflyg. One of the latter company's aircraft, SE-DNI, is seen here in LOT livery climbing out of Schiphol

Above Hungary's Malev became the first eastern European country to operate the 737 when, towards the end of 1988, it took delivery of three series -200s leased from Guiness-Peat. These have since been supplemented by three -300s from the same source. Illustrated soon after take-off from Schiphol is HA-LEB, a 737-2M8 previously operated by TEA Belgium

Left The latest eastern European state carrier to acquire 737 aircraft is Tarom of Rumania, who have just accepted delivery of the last of five 737-38J aircraft. The first of these was registered YR-BGA and named *Alba Lulia* – it is seen here taxying clear of the runway at Schiphol in October 1994

Above Icelandair operates one of the most modern fleets of any airline, comprising four Fokker 50s, four 737-400s and three 757s. Its fourth 737-408, TF-FID *Heiddis*, was delivered in April 1991, and photographed a year later at Glasgow's Abbotsinch airport

Right The People's Republic of China is now one of Boeing's largest customers, and it is estimated that about half of the company's manufacturing output for 1994 is destined for the Far East. Favourite choice of the Chinese airlines is without a doubt the 737, and China Southern Airlines alone operates some 40 'baby Boeings'. These mostly comprise the series -300s and -500s, and one of the latter is B-2547, a 737-5Y0 leased from Guiness-Peat and photographed at Hong Kong's Kai Tak airport

Above When the hermit nation of Burma changed its name to Myanmar, the national carrier, Union of Burma Airways, became Myanmar Airways. A joint venture between the national carrier and Highsonics Enterprise of Singapore has since produced a new start-up airline known as Myanmar Airways International. It initially operated a 757 leased from Royal Brunei, but now utilises a 737-400 leased from Malaysia Airlines. The aircraft concerned, 9M-MMH, flies from Yangon (formerly Rangoon) to several regional destinations, including Kai Tak, where it was photographed on final approach in November 1994

Right Seen on it's take-off roll from Kai Tak's runway 13 is Air China 737-3J6 B-2535. This airline is the national carrier, and operates a predominantly Boeing fleet of 707s, 737s, 747s and 767s

Above Thai Airways ceased to exist in 1988 when it was taken over by Thai International. At the time the company operated a small fleet of Shorts SD-330 and 360s, 737s and A310s. Illustrated at Bangkok in the company's seductive livery is 737-200 HS-TBD

Right After many years of operating ageing equipment Philippine Airlines recently began a modernisation programme which has seen Fokker 50s used on domestic routes, supplemented by 737s. This type is also used on some regional services, whilst two of four planned 747-400s are now in use on scheduled flights to the USA, leaving the ageing series -200 aircraft to serve Europe and Asia. The boring all-white fuselage of the company's aircraft helps to emphasise the inspiring tail livery as seen on 737-3S3 RP-C4006, about to land at Kai Tak

Above A new Asian carrier formed in 1992 is Cambodia International Airlines. From its base at Phnom Penh's Pochentong airport, the airline operates regional services using leased 1969-vintage 737-2E1 N197AL. The aircraft concerned is seen here about to land at Kai Tak

Right Now that it has taken delivery of the bulk of its A320 order, All Nippon Airways has completely disposed of its 737s to subsidiary Air Nippon. This photograph of 737-281 JA8452 was taken at Nagoya in April 1990 when in All Nippon service. As the type was used solely on domestic services the airline titles are in Japanese characters only

Above New Caledonie is a French protectorate, and as such its aircraft carry French registrations as seen on 737-33A F-ODGX of Air Caledonie, photographed taxying to its parking spot at Auckland, New Zealand

Right New generation variants of the 737 are proving popular with emerging airlines in the nations of Oceania. Of these Fiji-based Air Pacific has without a doubt one of the most paradisal schemes of any airline, as evidenced by this shot taken at Auckland of 737-5Y0 DQ-FJB *Island of Taveuni*

Above Air Vanuatu is the national carrier of the small island of the same name, and its fleet comprises a single EMB-110 Bandeirante and a 737-476. The latter aircraft, VH-TJI, is leased from Qantas. It was photographed about to land at Sydney in March 1993 in partial Australian Airlines livery. The aircraft was leased from the latter company, until it was taken over by Qantas

Above right Polynesian Airlines of Samoa operates a fleet of just four aircraft – a Britten-Norman BN-2 Islander, a DHC-6 Twin Otter and two 737-300s. Photographed at Auckland in the airline's balmy livery is 737-3Q8 5W-ILF. This machine was damaged recently when it was forced to land at its Apia base with the starboard undercarriage retracted. The malfunction was apparently caused by the body of a stowaway found afterwards in the undercarriage bay

Right Air New Zealand's fleet is comprised solely of Boeing products; the 737, 747 and 767. The 737 fleet now totals 12, most of which are 737-219 variants. All are named after birds found in New Zealand, and *Piwakawaka*, the Maori name for fantail, is allocated to ZK-NAS, seen here at Auckland

Above One could be forgiven for thinking this photograph of a TunisAir 727 and 737 was taken at Tunis airport, but it was in fact taken at Geneva in April 1992 – Tunisia is obviously a favourite destination for the Swiss. Both aircraft are wearing the new livery introduced in 1991. The airline has recently taken delivery of three 737-5H3 variants to supplement its four 737-2H3s, of which TS-IOC is illustrated

Left Photographed inbound to Heathrow on a rare crystal clear day is ST-AFL, one of two 737-2J8C variants operated by Sudan Air. This type is seldom seen at the London airport now, the Airbus A310 being preferred on the route

Boeing 747

The Boeing 747 – perhaps better known by its nickname the 'Jumbo' – took to the air for the first time on 9 February 1969 from Paine Field, the runway adjacent to the large production facility at Everett, Washington. This aircraft was joined by the next four production aircraft at Boeing Field, in the Seattle suburbs, for a 10-month long test programme during which over 1400 flying hours were accumulated. Initial recipient of the Jumbo was Pan American who, when they announced that they were to buy 25 747s at $21 million a copy, caused gasps of shock to reverberate round the head office of many an airline.

The airline launched its inaugural Jumbo service on 22 January 1970 on the prestigious 'Blue Ribbon' New York to London route. Whilst Pan Am's 747 network built up rapidly in a blitz of publicity, the second operator, Trans World Airlines, began much more cautiously with a New York - Los Angeles service, followed two months later by the New York - London route. The first foreign operator to commence 747 services was Lufthansa who, in April 1970, replaced its 707s on the Frankfurt - New York route. In the following months Air France and Alitalia started services from their respective capital cities to New York. By the end of 1970 a further seven operators, including Japan Airlines and Iberia, had taken delivery of 747s. Within a few years the 747-100, which could carry up to 516 passengers, took pride of place in the inventories of many national carriers.

One variant developed specially for Japan Airlines was the 747-100SR, the suffix standing for Short Range. The SR was designed for high density/short range sectors, with a typical flight duration of one hour or less. The cabin configuration of these aircraft is ten abreast in an all economy class, and this variant is also in use with All Nippon Airways. Although externally identical to other -100 series aircraft, the SR variant required strengthening of various items such as its undercarriage, due to the extraordinary high number of landings during the type's life cycle. The first SR – the 221st 747 built – first flew on 31 August 1973. The main production of the -100 series was terminated early in 1976, although a few for Saudia and a number of SR variants were produced during the 1980s. Including the prototype, a total of 207 series -100s were built, and despite most now being well over 20 years old, the majority are still in use today,

Left Framed by the towering blocks of flats built in the shadow of Lion Rock, a United Airlines 747-400 is captured on film moments before landing on runway 13 at Hong Kong's Kai Tak airport in November 1994

though increasing numbers are being converted into freighters.

Boeing quickly realised that the 747 was capable of improvement, particularly with the availability of more powerful engines. The company therefore strengthened the airframe and landing gear of the aircraft, thus enabling it to significantly increase the 747's maximum take-off weight and permit the customer to increase fuel or passenger capacity, and of course range – this variant was the -200B. It was identical dimensionally to the -100, although internally the upper deck is lengthened to increase capacity. The first 747-200 was the 88th Jumbo built, and in November 1970 it was delivered to Northwest Airlines, with whom it is still in use.

The -200 soon became the preferred variant of most airlines, particularly when other models such as the -200C Combi, -200C(SCD) and -200F freighter were made available. One lesser known model of the -200 is the -200(SUD), the letters standing for Stretched Upper Deck, which permits an

Above Wide-bodies abound! Only Tokyo's Narita airport has more flights of wide-bodied airliners in a day than Kai Tak. Here, a United 747-400 is lining-up on runway 13, whilst in the background 747-400s of China and Japan Airlines mingle with two Cathay Pacific Tristars and a China Eastern MD-11

Above Most of United Airlines 747-400 fleet now appear in the airline's new livery. Featured here is 747-422 N191UA, which was the 984th 747 built. It was delivered to the operator from Boeing's Everett plant in June 1993

increase in capacity. This variant is externally indistinguishable from the -300. KLM returned 10 of its -200 aircraft to the manufacturer to have this modification incorporated, which spurred Boeing to produce its next variant with this as standard, hence the 747-300. By the time production of the -200 was terminated a total of 393 had been built, including freighters.

To further increase capacity on the -300 a straight staircase to the upper deck replaced the spiral one, allowing the capacity of this section to be increased to 69, and giving a normal capacity of 538 passengers. Japan Airlines, however, was quick to take advantage of the increased room, and on its -300(SR) aircraft seat 563. The first -300 was rolled out on 15 September 1982, but due to the certification programme it was not delivered to customer Swissair until March the following year. This was the 570th Jumbo to leave the Everett production line.

The Boeing 747SP (Special Performance) is instantly recognisable from

Above Atlas Air Cargo is a New York-based air freight operator which was formed in 1992. Its fleet comprises four 747 freighters, including this aircraft, N3203Y, a 747-128F previously owned by Air France and photographed in October 1994 landing at New York's JFK airport. The tail logo features the mythological giant Titan who bore the heavens on his shoulders. The company uses the quaint radio callsign 'Giant'

Right In the first quarter of 1993 Air Canada unveiled a new livery which, like many others in the 1990s, is based on an all-white fuselage. The tail is dark green – although it looks almost black – upon which has been painted a vivid red maple leaf. Climbing into the clear blue skies over Toronto is 747-133 C-FTOD

its stable-mates by its somewhat stumpy appearance. This is due to the fuselage being reduced in length by 14.35 m (47ft 1 in), while the fin has been increased in height by 3.05 m (10 ft). The SP was designed for long range use on thinner long haul routes, thanks to a higher cruising speed and reduced fuel consumption. That great pioneer, Pan American, was the first customer for the SP model with an order for 10, and the first of the type, the 265th 747 built, took to the skies on 4 July 1975. Although it is in use as a VIP transport by the governments of Iraq, Oman, Saudi Arabia and the United Arab Emirates, the SP was not a great success. The production line was closed down in August 1982, although one further aircraft was subsequently built in 1987, taking total numbers to 44.

The latest variant of the 747 is the series -400, currently the world's largest, heaviest and most powerful airliner, and the only model of the Jumbo now in production. Soon after it was first announced in May 1985 orders literally poured in, and deposits had been paid on over 100 aircraft by the time the first one was rolled out on 26 January 1988. The fuselage of the -400 has the same dimensions of the -300, but that is where any similarity ends. For example, the wings are structurally redesigned with aluminium-lithium alloy skin panels, thus saving about 2722 kg (6000 lb) in weight, and the span is increased by 1.83 m (6 ft). The most striking features, however, are the two large 1.83 m (6 ft) high winglets which improve the aerodynamics of the aircraft. There are also additional fuel tanks in the horizontal tail which, added to the lighter wings wings, give a range increase of over 1000 miles compared to the -300. The manufacturer claims this model gives fuel savings of 24per cent over the earlier -200

Above Air Club International is a new Canadian charter operator which commenced transatlantic services in the summer of 1994 with two Airbus A310s and one 747. Although Montreal-based, the airline concentrated on services from Vancouver to Manchester and Gatwick, and has recently announced a major increase in services to Europe in 1995 which will also include Toronto

Above Due to severe financial problems, and its inability to meet lease payments, Varig has recently returned its three 747-400s. The airline has, however, retained eight earlier Jumbo variants on its inventory; three series -200s and five -300s. One of the latter, 747-341 PP-VOB, is illustrated at Rio de Janeiro's Galeao international airport

series. It also features a modern 'glass' cockpit, with analogue displays having been replaced by multi-coloured electronic displays which considerably reduce cockpit workload, and allow the aircraft to be operated by a two-man crew.

The maiden flight of the first -400, the 696th Jumbo built, took place on 29 April 1988, and although destined for launch customer Northwest Airlines, it was used in the type's certification programme. The honour of the first delivery to a customer therefore fell to VR-HOO, which was accepted by Cathay Pacific in Hong Kong on 28 August 1988. The -400 has proved an outstanding success, and it has already easily outsold the previous best-selling model, the -200.

This is quite an achievement considering that the -400 has been in service for just over six years. Not surprisingly the two major Japanese carriers operate an SR variant known as the -400(D) for domestic use, in which

Above The name *City of Birmingham* has been applied to British Airways 747-236B G-BDXJ, seen here taxiing past an Air New Zealand 747-419

Left The first aircraft to appear in Virgin Atlantic's revised livery is the airline's sole 747-123, registered G-VMIA and named *Spirit of Sir Freddie* after the legendary aviation entrepreneur Sir Freddie Laker. The revised livery involves the removal of the cheatline and, although not applied to this aircraft, bold silver titling on the cabin roof. In addition the engine cowlings are painted bright red too. This has prompted crews to call them BRTs (Big Red Things!)

configuration they can seat up to 569 passengers. This variant dispenses with the winglets as it is more cost effective without them on the short sectors involved.

A proud moment for Boeing and its Everett division occurred on 10 September 1993 with the roll-out of the 1000th 747, an aircraft destined for Singapore Airlines, one of the company's best customers. Boeing has also produced a dedicated freighter version, the -400F, which first entered service with Cargolux in late 1993. With the order book still bulging, it is perfectly conceivable that a figure of 1500 747s built could be achieved within the next decade, and with no suitably large successor even close to leaving the computer-generated 'drawing board', the 'Jumbo's' undisputed, and unofficial, title as 'king of the wide-bodies' should remain intact well into the next century.

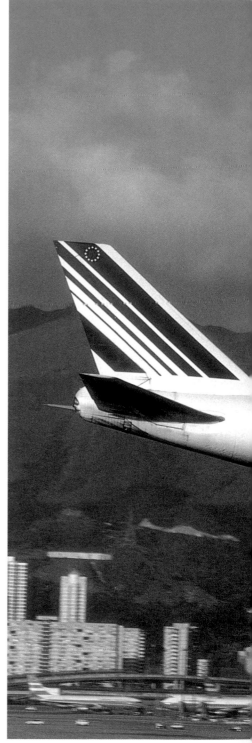

Above Air France now uses its -400 series aircraft on passenger services to Hong Kong. Making a final correction to line up with runway 13 at Kai Tak is 747-428 F-GISC – note that the red is missing from the airline's tail colours. The reason behind this is that F-GISC used to be operated by Air France Asie, a subsidiary formed for political reasons in order to allow the airline to operate both to Taipei and Beijing. The re-applied fuselage titling is further proof of its previous operator

Right Coming in for a landing at a crowded Kai Tak is Air France Cargo 747-228F freighter F-BPVV

Above Kuwait Airways has recently revised its livery slightly by reducing the width of the cheatline and dropping it below the window line. During the latter part of 1995 the airline will take delivery of two of the three 747-400s on order. Meanwhile, its four series -269Bs soldier on servicing Europe and New York. 9K-ADC, named *Al-Mubarakiya*, was seen at Heathrow in July 1994

Right Lufthansa is another major European airline which now operates the series -400 Jumbo to Hong Kong. The type's increased range allows European operators to offer non-stop services that bypass Middle East fuel stops such as Dubai, and thereby cut about two to three hours off the flying time. Framed by Lion Rock, Lufthansa's 747-430 D-ABTH *Duisburg* makes a stunning subject as it turns onto final approach for Kai Tak's runway 13

Left Cathay Pacific operates a large fleet of 747s, the first of which was delivered in 1980 for use on the long sought after route to London. The first two were series -267Bs, including VR-HIB which is seen here over densely populated Kowloon, inbound to Kai Tak.

Above Cathay Pacific unveiled its new livery on the airline's first Airbus A330 at the Farnborough Airshow in September 1994. Less than two months later the scheme appeared on 747-467 VR-HOT, an aircraft which was delivered to the airline back in September 1990

Above Asia is probably the only area of the world where the recession in the airline industry has not been felt, and this has been a major factor in the increasing number of 747-400s operated by the region's airlines, including Japan Airlines, China Airlines and Thai International

Right Another Kai Tak-based 747 operator is the cargo airline Air Hong Kong, which boasts a fleet of three freighters that all previously served with Federal Express. Seen here in the company's striking scheme is VR-HKO, a 747-249F which first entered service with the now-defunct Flying Tigers in September 1980 as N810FT

Above The major competitor to JAL is All Nippon Airways, whose sizeable fleet comprises over 50 767s and nearly 40 747s. As mentioned in the previous chapter, all its 737s have been transferred to subsidiary Air Nippon following their replacement by 20 A320s – all of the latter will have been delivered by December 1995. The airline is also in the process of deciding whether to defer or even cancel orders for both the A340 and Boeing 777. Photographed inbound to Kai Tak in All Nippon's vivid blue and white colour scheme is 747-281B JA8181

Right With the 'Dunlops' dangling, JAL's 747-446 JA8073 is seen on final approach to Kai Tak. The airline's rather staid livery features a grey nose-band with a red portion which looks not unlike a filtered cigarette!

Above China Airlines has four 747SPs on its inventory, but N4522V is the only one currently wearing the airline's colours – the others operate in the markings of subsidiary Mandarin Airlines

Right Korea's Asiana Airlines was formed as recently as 1988, and is already providing serious competition to the national carrier Korean Air. Asiana's fleet is comprised solely of Boeing products; the 737, 747 and 767. The first of three series -400 freighters have just been delivered to complement eight 747-48E passenger variants. Of the latter, HL7417 was accepted in December 1993, being the 1002nd 747 built

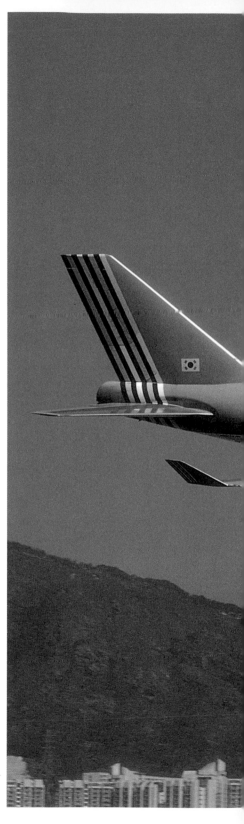

Above Singapore Airlines is the third-largest operator of the 747 after Japan Airlines and British Airways. The airline currently operates 24 series -412s, and has dubbed the variant 'Megatop'. The titling is displayed on the cabin roof above the upper deck windows, as seen on 9V-SMN which is lining up for take-off from Kai Tak

Above right Screaming over the Kowloon rooftops with Kai Tak's control tower in the background, Philippine Airlines 747-2F6B N743PR is just seconds away from completing yet another transpacific haul from the West Coast of America. It is one of four series -200s acquired during 1979/80, and whose numbers have since been swelled by a further seven aircraft from a number of leasing companies

Right During 1994 a number of Malaysia Airlines aircraft featured the bold 'Visit Malaysia Year 94' titles. This method of promoting tourism has been a regular feature of Asian airlines' liveries over the past decade. On this occasion it adorns 747-4H6 9M-MPA, one of 11 series -400 aircraft operated by Malaysia's national carrier

Above Qantas became the first airline in the world to operate an all-Boeing 747 fleet. It took delivery of its first series -200 Jumbo in September 1971, replacing the 707 – the last of these was disposed of in 1979, leaving the leviathan as the sole type in the inventory. Most of the -200s have now been disposed of, as have the two 747SPs which have been transferred to subsidiary Austasia. A few -300s soldier on alongside the 18 series -400s, however, the airline dubbing the latter variant 'Longreach'. Illustrated at Auckland, bound for Sydney, is VH-OJH *City of Darwin*

Above right This special colour scheme was unveiled on Qantas 747-438 VH-OJB in September 1994. Entitled *Wunala Dreaming* (Wunala is aborigine for Kangaroo), the scheme was devised to celebrate Australia's cultural heritage, and it is planned to use the aircraft on every route in the company's network. The aircraft performed a flypast at the 1994 Farnborough Airshow as a replica Vickers Vimy took-off to re-enact a flight to Australia. It also inaugurated Qantas services to Osaka's new Kansai airport

Right The Maori symbol Koru is prominent on the tail of Air New Zealand aircraft, in this case a 747-419.

Boeing 757

Although it first flew in February 1982, the concept of the 757 can be traced back to almost a decade earlier when Boeing identified the need to update the very successful 727-200 series. The proposed 727-300 failed to attract significant interest amongst the major airlines, with the aircraft's thirsty and noisy engines no doubt being the main contributing factor. A major rethink by the Boeing design team brought about the 7N7, with its broader fuselage cross-section and a completely redesigned wing. The 727 'T' tail was to be retained and the aircraft had a projected seating capacity in the range of 160 to 180 passengers. Although the 7N7 idea was better received by the airlines, there was resistance to the wider fuselage, particularly from those operating in the US domestic market. Boeing's designers returned to their drawing boards.

On paper the fuselage cross-section of the 727 was married to the new wing and engines, whilst the 'T' tail was dispensed with, and thus the 757 was born. Seating would be six abreast with a single isle, and the aircraft would be able to achieve a range of 4000 nm, enabling US carriers to fly non-stop coast to coast services. Formal announcement of the project came in February 1978 and, powered by two Rolls-Royce RB211 engines, the 757 was to be the first Boeing airliner launched by non-American engines. Pratt & Whitney PW2037 and 2040 engines became available at a later date, giving customers a choice of powerplant.

The basic variant is the 757-200, and launch orders were placed by Eastern and British Airways for 21 an 19 aircraft respectively, with options on further machines down the line. The 757s are produced alongside 737s at the company's Renton plant in the south-eastern suburbs of Seattle, and once an aircraft takes-off from Renton on its maiden flight it never returns, landing instead at nearby Boeing Field only some five miles away. Here, it completes its flight tests and fitting out to customer requirements.

Right Pre-delivery and research flight testing of a number of airliner types is undertaken at Boeing Field in the Seattle suburbs, which is also where 737s are painted. Seen on part of the ramp being readied for delivery are 757s for United, Condor and Britannia Airways, whilst in the distance a Royal Brunei 767 returns after undergoing a series of test flights

Above North American cousins – Air Transat 757-23A C-GTSE with a Continental 747-200

Right Established in the charter business for many years, Britannia Airways have won many accolades for their in-flight service, much of which was innovative for a charter operator. The airline has a modern Boeing fleet comprising 19 757s – deliveries of which were completed during 1994 – and nine 767s. Photographed rotating away from Gatwick is 757-204 G-BYAP

The prototype, appropriately registered N757A, was rolled out on 13 January 1982, and took to the air for the first time on 19 February, powered by two RB211-535C engines. By now the order book was growing as Delta had announced a commitment to 60 aircraft, and in turn become the first customer to specify Pratt & Whitney PW2037 engines. Hoped for orders from American carriers Air Florida and Aloha failed to materialise, however, although a modest, but nevertheless important ,order for two aircraft came from British charter airline Monarch. This proved to be the first of many from British charter airlines, and there are now more 757s on the British register than in the rest of Europe.

The first production aircraft was delivered to Eastern Airlines on 22 December 1982, and it commenced services on 1 January 1983. British Airways first 757 was delivered on 25 January 1983, with the type entering service on 9 February on the Heathrow - Belfast 'shuttle' service. The type soon replaced Tridents on other shuttle routes to Edinburgh, Glasgow and

Manchester, before being introduced on foreign routes. In BA service 757s are operated in two configurations – 195 economy seats on shuttle routes, and 180 seats in business/economy on European routes. The latter layout is fairly standard for most 757 operators, although in charter configuration some airlines seat as many as 233 passengers! Boeing have in fact made provision for a maximum of 239 passengers.

Boeing soon improved the product range in time-honoured fashion by offering two new models, the first being the extended range 757-200ER, three of which were ordered by Royal Brunei Airlines, and powered by Rolls-Royce RB211-535E4 engines, each with 40,100 lbs thrust. Secondly, as a result of enquiries from United Parcel Service a dedicated freighter version, the 757-200PF (Package Freighter) was announced in January 1986, coinciding with an order for 30 of the type by UPS. The model features a forward cargo door and is completely windowless. It can carry 15 standard cargo 'igloos', and the first of its type was delivered on 3 September 1987. In February 1986 the Combi variant was announced fitted with a cargo door, and it can be used in a mixed passenger/cargo configuration. Launch customer for this variant was Royal Nepal Airlines, whose Combi was delivered in September 1988, complementing a standard -200 delivered a year earlier.

Finally, in the late 1980s US carriers suddenly woke up to the fact that a world beater in the form of the humble 757 was being produced in their own backyard, and American Airlines, United and America West all placed substantial orders for the type. In Europe it seemed any self-respecting charter operator had to have 757s, with Air 2000, Britannia, Caledonian, Condor, LTE, LTU Sud and Transavia all operating the type. In China the 757 is also proving itself an ideal type for the emerging carriers in the region.

The 757 has proved virtually unsurpassed in fuel efficiency, and can climb higher and faster than any other single-aisle twin-jet – indeed, it is not uncommon for the type to cruise at 41,000 ft. Because of its impressive performance the 757 can use airports limited by runway length, high altitude, hot weather and weight restrictions, and that includes airfields which its baby brother, the 737-400, is unable to operate from. Such is the thrust available from the engines that operators of Rolls-Royce powered aircraft operate with the engines de-rated, yet the 757 is still one of the quietest airliners around. For charter operators its ETOPS (Extended Twin OPerationS) capability allows them to fly across the Atlantic, though adverse headwinds can force refuelling stops in places like Bangor.

The Boeing 757 has proved an exceptionally safe aircraft. In over ten years only one aircraft has been lost, and that was directly due to it being hit by another airliner while stationary on the ground. The jet in question was operated by CAAC (Civil Aviation Administration of China), and was

Above Airports which serve the major holiday resorts of the Mediterranean are the ideal places to see aircraft from charter airlines from all over Europe. Photographed at its Palma base is an LTE 757, framed by the tail of Air 2000's 757-225 G-OOOM

Right British Airways names its 757s after well known British castles, and *Kenilworth Castle* is allocated to 757-236 G-BIKZ. The long narrow fuselage is accentuated in this shot taken at Heathrow

at the holding point at Guanghzou awaiting take-off clearance when it was hit by an inbound 737 which was attempting to land after a hijacker had set off explosives.

At the time of writing almost 900 757s have been ordered, some 600 of which had been delivered.

Above Dutch airline Transavia operates both scheduled and inclusive tour charter flights using both 737s and 757s, with the latter being used predominantly for charter work. During the summer of 1994, 757-2K2 PH-TKC was decorated with soccer balls and the logo of the Dutch national team which took part in World Cup '94 in the USA

Above Another Dutch charter operator which flies both the 737 and 757 is Air Holland, the airline having two of each in their fleet. With reverse thrust selected, 757-27B PH-AHE decelerates after landing on runway 06 at Schiphol

Above Air Seychelles has used a 767-200ER on services to Europe since 1989 after it replaced an Airbus A300. In March 1993 the airline took delivery of a single 757-28A, registered S7-AAX and named *Aride.* The aircraft was acquired for new services, including Madrid, though unfortunately on its first visit to the Spanish capital it suffered damage at the hands, or should I say bumpers, of a ground-servicing vehicle

Left Spanish airline LTE uses a fleet of three 757s to convey tourists from northern Europe to the main Spanish resorts of Palma and the Canary Islands, and uses the appropriate radio callsign 'Funjet'. The airline is affiliated with German carrier LTU, hence the similarity in colour schemes. The aircraft featured, EC-EFX, is a 757-2G5 which previously served with LTU Sud as D-AMUR

Above Although unchanged for many years, Ethiopian Airlines has in my opinion one of the most attractive liveries of any operator. It is featured here on ET-AKC, one of four 757-260 aircraft currently in use. The company also operates a single 757-260PF freighter variant

Above left Xiamen Airlines is one of many Chinese operators of Boeing aircraft. These are primarily 737s, but also includes three 757s, one of which, B-2829, was photographed inbound to Kai Tak

Left There are now over 200 Boeing jetliners in use in the People's Republic of China. The best customer is without a doubt Guangzhou (Canton) based China Southern Airlines which has some 67 Boeings in its inventory. The ambitious carrier also has outstanding orders for both the Airbus A340 and Boeing 777. Photographed on the runway at Kai Tak is the airline's first 757-21B, B-2801, an aircraft which initially served in CAAC colours

Boeing 767

On 14 July 1978 Boeing announced that it was to proceed with the manufacture of the twin-engined 767 model following an order from United Airlines for 30 aircraft. Developed simultaneously with the 757, the 767 was aimed primarily at transcontinental and intercontinental routes. In appearance the 767 is similar to the Airbus A300, and is powered by two wing-mounted turbofan engines – the customer has a choice of General Electric, Pratt & Whitney or Rolls-Royce powerplants. The wide-body fuselage has twin-aisles with seven abreast seating in a 2x3x2 configuration, though this is often increased to 2x4x2 in charter configuration. The 767 is assembled in a building adjoining the 747 assembly hangar at Boeing's Everett plant, which shares the runway with Paine Field/Snohomish County airport.

The basic model is designated the 767-200, and the prototype was rolled out on 4 August 1981, with the first flight on 26 September – five months ahead of the 757 which is produced at Renton. By this time United had increased its order to 39 aircraft, with options for a further 30, whilst other US carriers in the form of American, Delta and TWA had ordered substantial numbers. By the end of 1981 Boeing had received 173 orders for the 767, with options on a further 138. These included commitments from across the border by Air Canada and Pacific Western, while All Nippon became the first Asian customer. Britannia Airways became the first European and also the first charter airline to select the type, followed quickly by Norway's Braathens. Inroads were made to South America when Colombia's Avianca joined those on the order book.

On 6 March 1984 the next variant, the 767-200(ER), flew for the first time. This aircraft features a higher gross weight and increased fuel capacity due to wing centre-section tanks, permitting a significant increase in range to over 4000 nm (6000 km). First recipient of this variant was Ethiopian

Left TWA, like Pan-American, was one of the pioneers of transatlantic jet travel. Nowadays the financially-troubled airline's fleet and routes are but a fraction of what they used to be. Most transatlantic routes are operated by 767-231(ER) aircraft like N650TW, which is captured on film at the point of rotation from Schiphol's runway 24

Above The TWA fleet now boasts just 12 747s, all but two of which are veteran series -100 aircraft., plus three recently acquired secondhand 767-300(ER)s to supplement the 767-200(ER) fleet on international services. Two of those are former Aer Lingus 767-3YO(ER) aircraft, including EI-CAL seen here about to land at New York's JFK airport. The letters TWA stand for Trans World Airlines, though there are those who say it really means 'try walking across'! Personally, on the three occasions I have flown with the airline I wish I had!

Right One of the most interesting colour schemes is that of TransBrasil. Although the company's livery features an all-white fuselage, this is more than compensated for by the tail which is completely covered in a series of blue, green, yellow, orange and red vertical stripes. On the 767 fleet this is taken a stage further with each aircraft having the wings painted a different colour. Although not really visible in this view at Rio's Galeao airport 767-2Q4 PT-TAA has blue wings

Above right The most successful American carrier at the moment is United Airlines, which has ridden the storm of recession in the airline industry. Intercontinental services are undertaken by 747s and 767s, with the latter being used predominantly on transatlantic routes. Wearing the airline's old livery inbound to Heathrow is 767-322(ER) N650UA

Airlines, who had placed the first 767 order from the African continent. The availability of the -200(ER) encouraged a number of airlines, including American and United, to switch some of their orders to the newer variant. In 1986 the 767-200(ER) set two new world records, the first being a new distance record of 6854 nm set up during the delivery of a Kuwait Airways aircraft from Seattle direct to the capital of the small Arab country. This was followed five months later when a Lan-Chile 767(ER) made the first scheduled crossing of the Atlantic by a twin-jet aircraft, completing the flight from Rio de Janeiro to Madrid in 10 hours 12 minutes.

In 1983 Boeing announced that a stretched variant, known as the series -300, was to be produced, with two fuselage plugs increasing the length by 6.43 m (21 ft 1 in) allowing capacity to be increased by 37 in maximum configuration. The first of this variant was delivered to Japan Airlines in September 1985, with competitor All Nippon taking delivery nearly two years later. The series -300(ER) extended range variant first flew on 19 December 1986, with American Airlines acting as launch customer – they have since put the type to use on an increasing number of transatlantic routes. The 767 family of aircraft, particularly the -300 variants, are proving increasingly popular with European charter airlines also due to their exceptional range and high density seating.

One of the attractions of the 767 is its ETOPS capability, which makes it an ideal choice for those who operate aircraft on long over water routes. Such is the reliability of modern airliners and engines that the 767 has been instrumental in changing the rules governing such flights by twin-engined aircraft. Previously, these twin-engined aircraft had to fly circuitous routes that would keep them within one hour's flight of an airport in case of the loss of an engine, a rule that does not apply to three and four-engined aircraft. However, the reliability of aircraft like the 757/767/A310 convinced the authorities that this figure should be extended to two hours. This approval was originally restricted to 767s powered by Pratt & Whitney JT9D-7R4 engines. However, it has since been extended to General Electric CF6-80A and Rolls-Royce RB211-535E engines. There are now a number of airframe/engine combinations and operators approved for ETOPS, many of which are cleared for flights up to three hours from land.

In 1995 the latest 767 variant will take to the air, this being the -300(ER) freighter for United Parcel Service, who have ordered an initial batch of 30, with options for a further 30. Boeing recently announced that production of the -200 variants has ceased, but there is no doubt that the popular -300 models will remain in production for a number of years yet and, at the time of writing, over 500 767s have been delivered to over 70 airlines worldwide.

Above right Photographed seconds away from touchdown at Las Palmas is Martinair 767-31A(ER) PH-MCG. The airline has recently changed its titling simply to Martinair, having previously carried the sobriquet Martinair Holland on its jets. However, when this aircraft was parked at the terminal gate the jetty covered part of the titling so that only 'AIR Holland', the name of a competitor, was visible!

Below right The subdued white scheme on Spanair's 767-3YO(ER) EC-FHA is offset by the threatening skies of a British spring day

Above Climbing out with another load of happy holidaymakers is Britannia Airways 767-204 G-BNCW. The airline operates nine 767s, including ER variants, and these venture as far afield as Australia and New Zealand. Britannia has also ordered four series -300(ER)s

Above left British Airways fleet of 23 767-336(ER) aircraft are used primarily to service routes to the Middle East, as well as a few US destinations. They are also utilised on some high density short sector European routes such as Heathrow - Paris, a flight of less than one hour's duration. Apart from three aircraft operated from Birmingham and Manchester, the aircraft are named after European cities. The airline's first 767 G-BNWA is named *City of Brussels*

Left Following British Airways investment in and subsequent code-share agreement with,USAir, a few of the latter's 767-200(ER) aircraft now operate in BA colours. These aircraft are presently used on services from London Gatwick to Baltimore, Charlotte and Pittsburgh. USAir has, however, recently announced that it plans to sell its 767s in an effort to raise badly needed cash. The registration N652US of this 767 in BA livery gives a big clue to as to its ownership

Above Balkan Bulgarian Airlines is another eastern European operator which, alongside LOT and Malev, uses 767s on transatlantic services. Two 767-27E(ER) aircraft are leased from Air France, of which F-GHGE is seen about to land on runway 31R at New York's JFK airport

Above right Lift-off! Wearing Air Aruba markings, 767-204(ER) ZK-NBI lifts off from Schiphol's runway 24. Air Aruba has used several leased 767s for its Aruba - Amsterdam service, including aircraft of Britannia Airways and Air New Zealand

Right Gulf Air now operates 20 767-3P6(ER)s, which are used on most of its international services. The airline has recently inaugurated a new route to New York with the first of its Airbus A340s. Poised to land on runway 13 at Kai Tak is A40-GV – the 502nd 767 built – delivered to the airline in June 1993

Above Israel's El Al has long been a proponent of Boeing products, and the airline's current fleet is comprised exclusively of products from Washington state, namely the 737, 747, 757 and 767 – there are four of the latter, two of which are extended range variants. One of those, 767-258(ER) 4X-EAC, is seen here about to depart London's Heathrow airport in June 1993

Above right Although it still has two 707s, Air Zimbabwe uses a pair of 767s acquired in 1989 and 1990 on its European routes. Finished in the airline's symbolic livery is the Z-WPF – the second 767-2NO(ER) – named *Chimanimani.* The company's other 767 is named *Victoria Falls*

Right To supplement its growing 747-400 fleet Asiana has three -300 and five -300(ER) variants in use, with a further five and two respectively on order. The aircraft illustrated, HL7268, is a 767-38E(ER) delivered in February 1992 and leased from ILFC

Boeing 777

In response to operator interest for a new airliner with a capacity between the 767-300 and the 747-400, Boeing came up with the 777. Formal announcement of the launch of the type was announced on 29 October 1990, two weeks after United Airlines had placed an order for 34, with options for a further batch of a similar number.

The wide-bodied 777 is the world's largest twin-jet, and features an interior cross-section greater even than current wide-body tri-jets. With twin-aisles, the seating can vary from six to ten abreast, depending on configuration, thus giving a capacity of up to 328 in a three class layout. In two class fit this will rise to 400, and in an all-economy layout as many as 440. Initially, two variants will be offered, the A and B, also known as the -200 and -200(ER). The former will be suitable for domestic, regional and some international routes, and boast a range in the region of 3000 to 5000 nm, whilst the B-model, with a range in the region from 5000 to 7000 nm, is ideal for intercontinental routes such as transatlantic services.

Typical routes for the A-model would be New York - London and Chicago - Honolulu, whilst for the B-model New York - Bahrain and

Left Airborne! The prototype of the world's largest twin-jet climbs out on an early test flight. Note the insignia of customer airlines underneath the window line on the forward fuselage (*Boeing Airplane Company*)

Above Inside the huge assembly hangar at Boeing's Everett plant the completed forward fuselage of the prototype 777 is being moved into position for mating with centre and rear fuselage sections *(Boeing Airplane Company)*

Chicago - Seoul are perfectly viable. Both versions will have identical external dimensions, although the latter will have a higher gross weight, more powerful engines and additional fuel tanks. A stretched version is currently being studied and may be available from around 1998 onwards. Propulsion units offered are the General Electric GE90, Pratt & Whitney 4000 or Rolls-Royce Trent series engines, which will be as quiet as the powerplants used on the 767, despite offering 40 per cent more thrust.

There was some concern about the wing span which, although shorter than that of the 747-400, is longer than any other aircraft in service. United were concerned that the type would not be able to operate into airports with gates and taxyways designed around aircraft of DC-10 size. Boeing then came up with the innovative, for commercial aircraft at least, option of a folding wing about 6.8 m (22 ft) from the wingtip. However, no airline has yet taken up this option, no doubt because of the additional weight incurred. The modern two-crew flightdeck was designed around that of the 747-400. Like its other products Boeing has ensured the 777 can carry a healthy load of cargo in the underfloor hold – all told the 777 can accommodate a maximum of 32 standard LD-3 containers, plus 17 cu m (600 cu ft) of bulk loaded cargo for total lower hold volume of 160.1 cu m (5656 cu ft).

Following United, the next order for the 777 came from All Nippon Airways in December 1990 with commitment to purchase 15, and with options on 10. Next came the first European (charter) operator, Euralair of France, who placed orders for two B-models in June 1991. These were soon followed by orders from Thai International, British Airways and Lauda Air. During 1992 Japan Airlines, Cathay Pacific, Emirates and China Southern were added to the list, as was the first leasing company, ILFC. These were followed in 1993 with orders from Japan Air System, Gulf Air, TransBrasil and Korean Air. By 30 March 1994 a total of 147 orders and 108 options had been taken from 15 airlines and one leasing company.

Wearing the Boeing red, white and blue house colours the prototype was rolled out from the Everett plant on 9 April 1994, and took to the air on its maiden flight on 12 June. That premier trip lasted for three hours and 48 minutes, and was the first of 4800 test flights planned by nine aircraft in the flight test programme. From this point on things progressed rapidly, and the fourth 777 took to the air on 28 October 1994.

The 777 is well on the way to achieving its target of first delivery of a 777-222 to United on 15 May 1995. The aircraft is planned to enter service the following month, probably on the Denver - Honolulu route.

Technical Specifications

	707-320C	727-200	737-400	747-400
First flight date:	19 February 1963	27 July 1967	19 February 1988	29 April 1988
Maximum accommodation:	219	189	170	569
Wing span:	44.42 m (145 ft 9 in)	32.92 m (108 ft 0 in)	28.88 m (94 ft 9 in)	64.31 m (211 ft 0 in)
Length:	45.60 m (152 ft 11 in)	46.96 m (153 ft 2 in)	36.40 m (119 ft 7 in)	70.66 m (231 ft 10 in)
Height:	12.94 m (42 ft 5 in)	10.36 m (34 ft 0 in)	11.13 m (36 ft 6 in)	19.33 m (63 ft 5 in)
Max t/o weight:	151,315 kg (333,600 lb)	95,027kg (209,500 lb)	68,040 kg (150,000 lb)	397,000 kg (875,000 lb)
Range with max. pax.:	7408 km (4000 nm)	4043 km (2464 nm)	4104 km (2505 nm)	13,528 km (8406 nm)

	757-200	767-300(ER)	777-200B
First flight date:	18 February 1982	19 December 1986	12 June 1994
Maximum accommodation:	239	327	440
Wing span:	38.05 m (124 ft 10 in)	47.57 m (156 ft 1 in)	60.90 m (199 ft 11 in)
Length:	47.32 m (155 ft 3 in)	54.94 m (180 ft 3 in)	63.72 m (209 ft 1 in)
Height:	13.56 m (44 ft 6 in)	15.85 m (52 ft 0 in)	18.44 m (60 ft 6 in)
Max. t/o weight:	113,295 kg (250,000 lb)	184,640 kg (407,000 lb)	263,090 kg (580,000 lb)
Range with max. pax.:	7408 km (4000 nm)	11,230 km (6060 nm)	11,170 km (6030 nm)